RUNNING WILD

RUNNING WILD

AWESOME ANIMALS IN MOTION

WRITTEN BY
GALADRIEL WATSON

ART BY
SAMANTHA DIXON

annick press
toronto • berkeley

Cover art by Samantha Dixon, designed by Paul Covello
Designed by Paul Covello
Thank you to Kim Ryall Woolcock, BSc, MA, for the expert review.

Annick Press Ltd.

We acknowledge the support of the Canada Council for the Arts and the Ontario Arts Council, and the participation of the Government of Canada/la participation du gouvernement du Canada for our publishing activities.

Library and Archives Canada Cataloguing in Publication

Title: Running wild : awesome animals in motion / written by Galadriel Watson ; art by Samantha Dixon.
Names: Watson, Galadriel, author. | Dixon, Samantha, illustrator.
Identifiers: Canadiana (print) 20190198117 | Canadiana (ebook) 20190198125 | ISBN 9781773213705 (hardcover) | ISBN 9781773213699 (softcover) | ISBN 9781773213736 (PDF) | ISBN 9781773213729 (Kindle) | ISBN 9781773213712 (HTML)
Subjects: LCSH: Animal locomotion—Juvenile literature. | LCSH: Animal mechanics—Juvenile literature.
Classification: LCC QP301 .W38 2020 | DDC j573.7/9343—dc23

Published in the U.S.A. by Annick Press (U.S.) Ltd.
Distributed in Canada by University of Toronto Press.
Distributed in the U.S.A. by Publishers Group West.

Printed in China

annickpress.com
galadrielwatson.com
samdixon.ca

Also available as an e-book. Please visit annickpress.com/ebooks for more details.

INTRODUCTION

MARVELOUS MOTION

The kangaroo hops huge distances—but never gets tired.

The flea is as small as a pencil-point—but jumps high up to the back of a passing dog.

The albatross rarely flaps its wings—but soars in the air for hours.

The fishing spider is as big as an adult person's palm—but walks on top of the lake.

Animals of all shapes and sizes must move—their lives depend on it. They need to find food, or escape from becoming food. They need to mate. They may need to migrate or defend their territories. Whatever the reasons, animals are always traveling from place to place, and they do so in many amazing ways.

In this book, you'll meet a collection of animals that move differently. You'll meet those that live on land, in air, and in water. Those that use feet, fins, or feathers to walk, swim, or fly. You'll learn about movements powered by muscles, waving hairs, or flowing liquids.

Some of these animals are the best at what they do—like the can't-catch-me cheetah or the wrist-twisting gibbon. Others are wonderful examples of the travel techniques of lots of similar animals—like the wing-flapping Canada goose or the fin-undulating triggerfish. Yet others seem utterly bizarre—like the slime-slipping snail or the rocket-booster squid—but make perfect sense for how the animal lives. Overall, you'll discover the main methods animals use to get from one spot to another.

MAY THE FORCE BE (MOSTLY) WITH YOU

No matter how fantastic animal movements appear, they can all be explained by science. The study of motion is called mechanics. It's called biomechanics when applied to living creatures.

Whether it's an airplane or albatross, the same rules apply. To start or stop movement, an object—including a living body—needs to be pushed or pulled. This push or pull is called a force. The object also needs to fight forces that are trying to move it in the wrong direction.

For example, let's look at the four major forces that affect how a bird flies.

Force #1: Gravity
Earth's pull tries to tug the bird down.

Force #2: Lift
To fight the gravity, the bird flaps its wings to create lift. This holds the bird up.

Force #3: Drag
Air seems easy to travel through, but it's actually not—think how hard it is to walk on a super windy day. This drag creates friction against the bird's body, which resists its forward movement, tries to push the bird backward, and tends to slow it down.

Force #4: Thrust
To fight the drag, the bird uses the power of its wings to create thrust, which pushes the bird forward.

Animals on land or in water also have to deal with similar forces. One force wants to pull it down—the animal has to work to stay up. Another force wants to drag it back—the animal has to work to move ahead. The animals also have to work with and against forces like friction and buoyancy. That's a lot of work!

In the following pages, you'll learn how animals manage to fight—and use—these forces to travel, along with unique methods and super-well-adapted body parts.

An astounding variety of creatures live on Earth—with an astounding variety of ways to move.

Want to discover some of them? Turn the page and hop to it!

CHAPTER ONE
LAND CROSSINGS
WALKING, RUNNING, AND HOPPING

Walking may seem like a boring way for a person to travel, but it's actually cool. Really.

That's because humans walk unlike any other creature. Sure, some other animals walk on two legs, like chimpanzees or birds. But when their feet hit the ground, their knees stay bent. We keep ours relatively straight. If we bent our legs, our thigh muscles would need to use more energy to get us moving. Instead, we take the straighter, more energy-efficient way. Aren't we smart!

Other animals have their own super savvy ways to travel across land—while working with and against forces like gravity and friction. The goal is to stay upright, balanced, and on the move. Tortoises live pretty casual lives, so their movements are rrrreeeaaalllyyy ssssllllooowww. Cheetahs have dinner to catch, so they're super fast. Kangaroos hop sort of like how humans run—with the bonus that they rarely get tired.

Let's take a saunter ...

SLOW-MO MOVER

The slope is rocky, and the tortoise is slow. It plods along, its thick, scaly legs taking turns lifting, swinging forward, and stepping down. Whoops, watch out! The creature wobbles and nearly falls. Then it steadies itself and, inch by inch, gradually moves ahead.

THE TIPPY TORTOISE

Tortoises are naturally slow movers. On the good side, moving slowly means their super strong muscles don't use much energy. On the bad side, if a tortoise starts to wobble, it can't move its legs very fast to keep itself upright. To stop gravity from toppling it, a tortoise may move only one leg at a time and balance on the other three, like a three-legged stool. Or it may lift the front leg on one side and the back leg on the opposite side and balance its weight between the two that remain on the ground. But if its balance isn't so good—oops!—the shell on its underside may hit the dirt.

HIDE ME!

Because of its less-than-impressive speed, a tortoise can't run from predators and other dangers. Instead, it hides in its handy shell. Depending on the type of tortoise, it may pull its head right inside the shell or fold its head to the side under the edge. When tucked back, its thick, scaly legs act like armored doors. Some types of tortoises can even clamp their upper and lower shells together. The pancake tortoise has a flat shell that lets it squeeze between rocks to keep safe. It then inflates its lungs to expand its body and **wedge** itself in, which means a predator will have a tough time pulling the tortoise out from its hiding place.

A **wedge** is a tool that is thicker at one end and thinner at the other. It can be used to separate an object (like how an ax head separates wood) or hold another object still (like how a doorstop keeps a door in place).

THAT EXTRA STRETCH

Tortoise shells can be shaped differently depending on the species' needs. Galápagos tortoises live on the Galápagos Islands in the Pacific Ocean near Ecuador. The ones that evolved in dry areas with little vegetation have "saddleback" shells that curve away from their necks. This extra room allows them to stretch their heads high to snatch hard-to-reach food. Galápagos tortoises that evolved in wetter areas with more easy-to-reach vegetation don't need this extra curve; they have "domed" shells instead.

MASTERS AT FLIPPING

Animals like turtles, beetles, and crabs have to be able to flip themselves over when they land on their backs. Dome-shelled Galápagos tortoises and many other types flail their heads and feet until their bodies rock enough to flip over. Other tortoises, including saddleback-shelled Galápagos tortoises, flail *and* extend their necks to push their heads against the ground. This neck-head motion acts as a **lever**, helping the tortoise return right-side up.

A **lever** is a rigid item like a rod that pivots at a fixed point, making it easier to move heavy things. Think of a shovel: to dig up a heavy clump of dirt, you force the shovel blade into the ground and then push down on the shovel's handle to pop up the dirt.

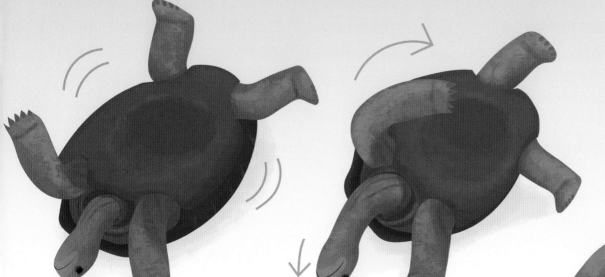

THE FASTEST BY FAR

Over the hot African grasslands, there's a blur of motion and a cloud of dust: a cheetah races toward its prey. Just look at that spine, that chest, that tail, that gaze, that grip on the ground! With a final burst of speed, the cheetah grabs the gazelle.

GET THAT GRIP

To move, animals like cheetahs (and humans) push against the ground with their feet. In turn, the ground pushes the animal's body forward. But this only works if there's strong contact between the ground and the feet—in other words, good friction. If the surface is slippery, like ice, the animal doesn't get very far. As the fastest land animal in the world, the cheetah relies on great friction. Although a sprinting cheetah places only one foot at a time on the ground, the paw stays firmly gripped to the earth thanks to two features: its pads, which are ridged and hard like tire treads, and its claws, which stick out a bit and poke into the ground like soccer cleats. With a solid grip, the cat can really push off.

BUILT FOR SPEED

A cheetah doesn't have as much muscle as other big cats, like lions—but it can run faster. One reason is that its thin, light body requires less power to move. It also has a big heart that pumps more energy-giving blood, and an extra-large nasal cavity and lungs that draw in more oxygen. Plus, its extraordinarily flexible S-shaped spine—like a human's, but even more flexible—stretches with each bound like a **spring**, which helps the cheetah leap even farther. To increase its speed, the cat moves its legs faster and increases the distance it covers with each stride (unlike the second-fastest land animal, a greyhound, which only increases the distance).

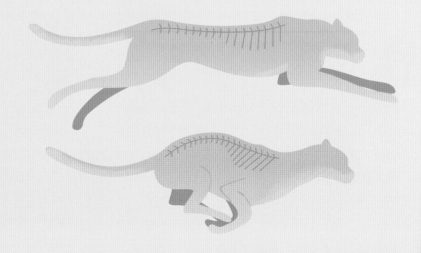

TIGHT TURNS

A gazelle can't run as fast as a cheetah, so it zigzags to try to lose its predator. To make sharp turns, the cheetah uses its tail somewhat like a **rudder**—if the cat whips its tail to one side, the animal will rapidly turn in the other direction. The tail also helps the cat stay balanced against gravity while turning, speeding up, and stopping.

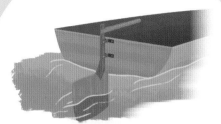

A **rudder** is a moving part used to steer an object like a boat.

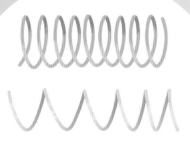

A **spring** is an object that returns to its original shape after being squished or stretched.

KEEPING TRACK

Cheetahs are amazing at keeping their eyes fixed on their prey. Even while they run at incredible speeds, they hold their heads still. Like humans, a cheetah has **organs in its inner ear** that tell it whether its head is moving up or down, is turned to the side, or is tilted. A cheetah's inner ear is extra big, so it can always control its head and watch its prey.

NONSTOP HOP

Like a bouncing ball, the kangaroo goes boing-boing-boing. Over clumps of grass and past trees to a watering hole, the kangaroo springs off its hind legs. Faster and faster it goes, with longer and longer bounds. Does it ever get tired? No!

A SPRING IN ITS STEP

Kangaroos hop—but rarely get tired. They first use muscle power to create thrust and fight gravity. Then, to keep going, they rely on the **super long and stretchy tendons** (the tissues that connect muscle to bone) in their hind legs. These act like springs, storing energy when the kangaroo lands and then releasing that energy to help the kangaroo jump away again. Humans run in a similar way, but our tendons aren't nearly as long. This means we have to use more muscle power, which can be exhausting!

A LEG UP

A kangaroo uses its tail in a way no other animal does—as an extra leg. When moving slowly, the kangaroo "walks" in two phases. First, it puts its weight on its front paws and its tail. Second, it swings its back legs forward. The tail isn't just used for balance but actually pushes against the ground to propel the animal ahead. Male kangaroos also lean on their tails so they can kick when fighting.

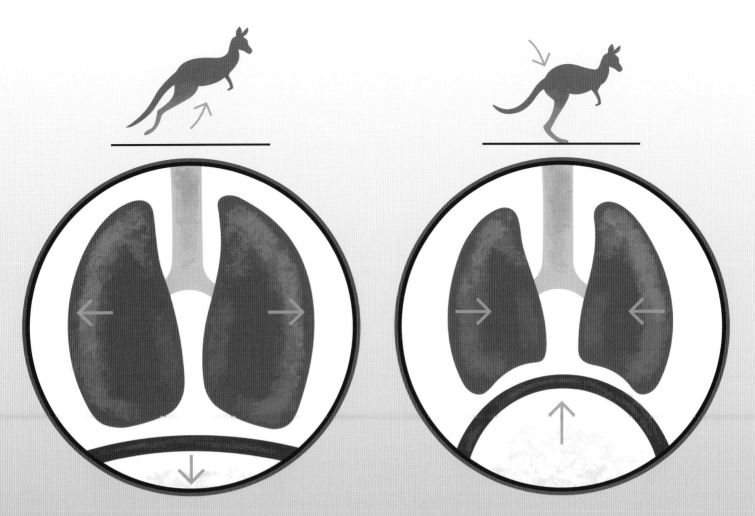

BREATHING EASY

There's another reason kangaroos stay energetic when hopping: this movement helps them breathe. Humans and other creatures have to use muscles to expand and contract their lungs to breathe. So do kangaroos when they're relatively still. But when they're hopping, **the organs in their abdomens flop around,** which inflates and deflates their lungs automatically.

LESSONS TO LEARN

Because kangaroo hopping is so effective, it was one of the inspirations that led to prosthetic legs for runners and other athletes. Prosthetic legs and feet that are made to look like real legs and feet don't provide any energy to get the person moving. By mimicking the springy tendons of kangaroos and other animals—and ditching the true-to-life look—prosthetics can now help athletes generate thrust and build speed.

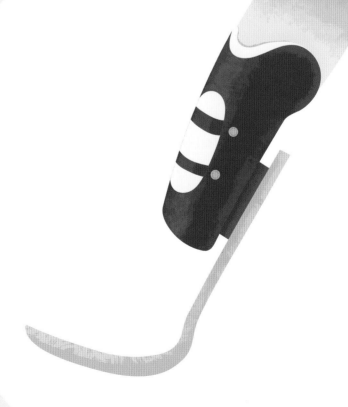

CHAPTER TWO
KEEPING A LOW PROFILE
CRAWLING

You've now met creatures that walk, run, and hop—but there are other ways to travel across solid surfaces. One example is crawling.

The palms of our hands and our knees would get pretty sore awfully fast if we spent too much time on them. But other animals are made to move down low—and their forms of crawling may look nothing like ours. In fact, when a creature crawls, it simply means that its body is super close to the ground or even touches it if the animal doesn't have legs. All that rubbing can make the force of friction a big deal—and provide a surprise advantage.

Crawling can take many forms. With their teeny legs, caterpillars take oodles of tiny steps. Snails use concealed waves that slip them forward over slime. You've likely seen how a snake slithers—but did you know there are several slithering methods? And amoebas . . . Wait a minute . . . what the heck is an amoeba? You'll find out soon.

Read on to learn the secrets of crawling—for both bigger creatures and mysterious single-celled critters.

LIFE ON A LEAF

Up the stem, over the twig, under the leaf. The little caterpillar crawls upside down, right-side up, and diagonally—eating constantly to grow into a healthy moth or butterfly. But how does it move without bones? How does it hang on?

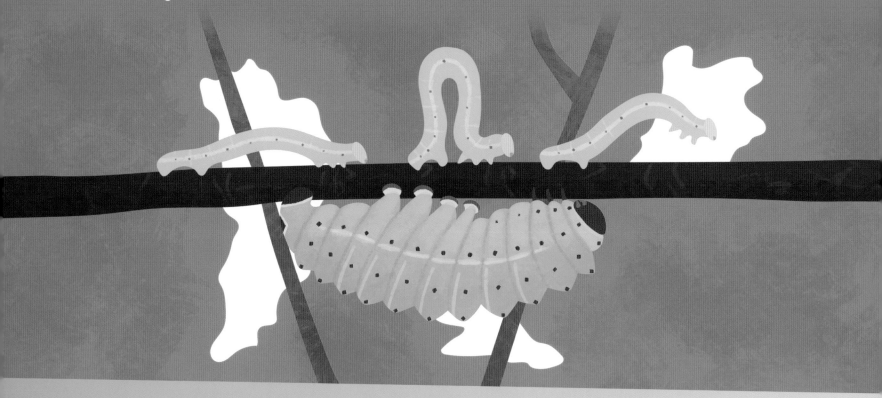

INCHING AHEAD

Caterpillars generally use two movements: crawling and inching. To crawl, a caterpillar's many sets of legs move in a wavy pattern of minuscule steps. To inch, the caterpillar brings its rearmost legs way forward, arching its back high into the air. Then it moves its front legs forward to stretch out again. Like humans, a caterpillar uses muscles to move, but instead of pulling against bone (which caterpillars don't have), the muscles pull against whatever surface the insect's attached to.

LOTS AND LOTS (AND LOTS) OF LEGS

Like all insects, a caterpillar has only six legs. Hold on—don't caterpillars have way more? Not really. Its front six legs are its true legs, the ones a larva keeps when it becomes a butterfly or moth. The rest of the stubby limbs are called prolegs, and they're used for inching or crawling. The number of prolegs and where they're located on its body depend on what type of caterpillar it is.

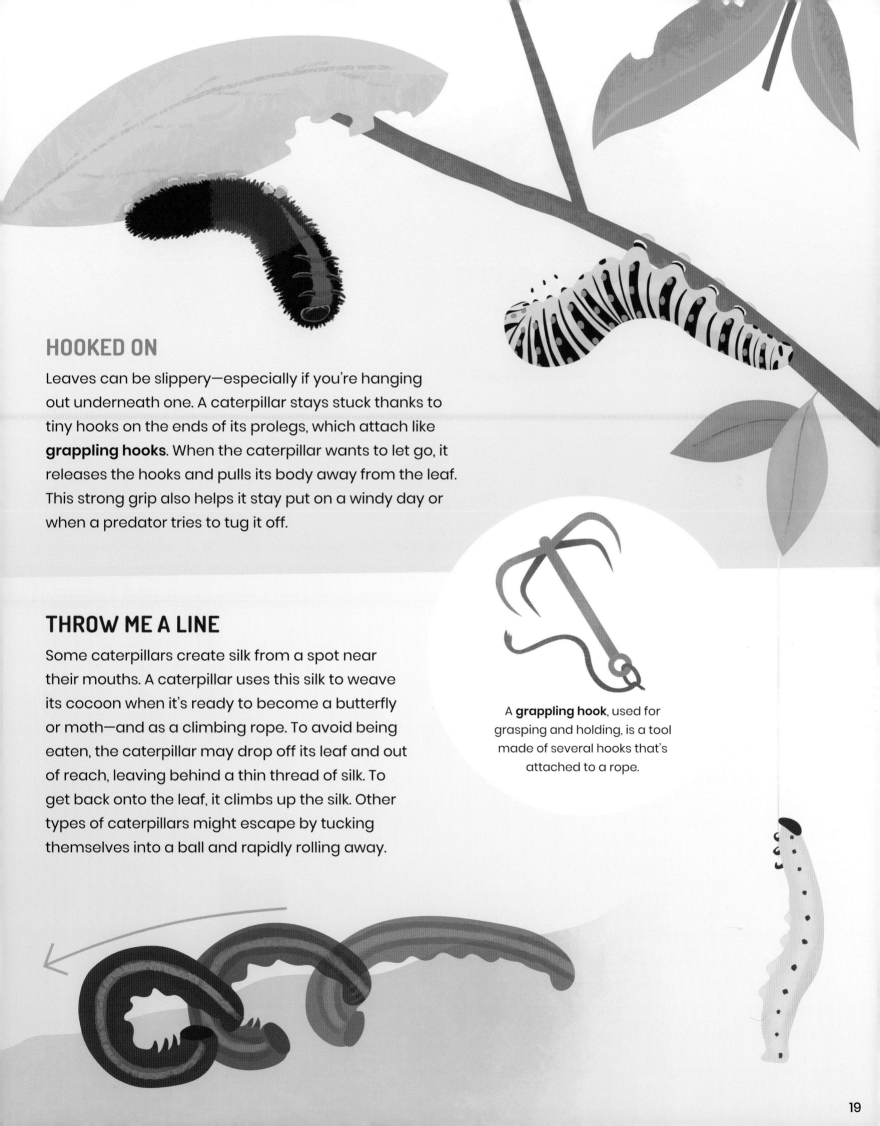

HOOKED ON

Leaves can be slippery—especially if you're hanging out underneath one. A caterpillar stays stuck thanks to tiny hooks on the ends of its prolegs, which attach like **grappling hooks**. When the caterpillar wants to let go, it releases the hooks and pulls its body away from the leaf. This strong grip also helps it stay put on a windy day or when a predator tries to tug it off.

THROW ME A LINE

Some caterpillars create silk from a spot near their mouths. A caterpillar uses this silk to weave its cocoon when it's ready to become a butterfly or moth—and as a climbing rope. To avoid being eaten, the caterpillar may drop off its leaf and out of reach, leaving behind a thin thread of silk. To get back onto the leaf, it climbs up the silk. Other types of caterpillars might escape by tucking themselves into a ball and rapidly rolling away.

A **grappling hook**, used for grasping and holding, is a tool made of several hooks that's attached to a rope.

SLIMY, SLIPPERY, AND STUCK

Like a ghost, the snail seems to float across the sidewalk. It has no legs and doesn't slither like a snake. Other than its tentacles—its eyes perched high on top of the tallest two—nothing seems to move. Behind it, a trail of slime glistens in the sun.

A BIG FLAT FOOT

Snails belong to a group of animals called gastropods, which means "stomach foot." That's because a snail's belly, on the underside of its body, is also its foot. Unlike a human foot, which lifts up, the snail's foot always stays flat on the ground. While most of the foot stays put, the snail uses its muscles to slide parts of it ahead a bit at a time. Very, very leisurely, the snail creeps along.

MAGICAL MUCUS

That trail of slime—called mucus, just like in your nose—is extremely important to a snail. For the parts of the snail's foot that are gliding ahead, the mucus acts slippery, reducing the friction that might hold it back. For the parts staying still, the mucus behaves like glue to provide friction. Like a **ratchet**, the mucus stops the snail from slipping backward by mistake and lets the animal slowly but steadily move forward.

A **ratchet** is a tool that allows movement in one direction only.

LEAPING TO SAFETY

Snails are slow—except when they're leaping! Many snails have an extra bit, called an operculum, attached to their feet. When they withdraw into their shells, this bit seals the opening and keeps them safe inside (like how a tortoise's legs help seal up its shell). A conch snail, however, uses its operculum in a different way. When threatened, this saltwater snail slams its operculum onto the seafloor, which makes it jump. It may do this maneuver again and again to hop out of harm's way.

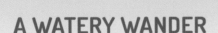

A WATERY WANDER

Some freshwater snails can walk on water—both underwater and upside down! These snails have air in their shells, which allows them to float at the top. The snail's foot then makes little ripples in the water's surface tension. Surface tension refers to how the water molecules on the surface stick tightly together, making it strong, almost like a layer of plastic wrap. The snail can then grip on to these ripples and use them to get moving.

WEAVING WAYS TO MOVE

The snake's head weaves from side to side as the animal slithers across the ground. But that isn't the only place suitable for a snake. In water, up in trees, or down in burrows, snakes live in a variety of locations and need to be able to move in a variety of ways.

FULL SLITHER AHEAD

Most of the time, a snake travels by forming its body into S-shaped waves. But if the ground is smooth, the snake can't go anywhere—there's not enough friction between its body and the ground. To move, the snake needs to push off things like stones or tufts of grass or catch on things like the tiniest bumps on the ground. A swimming snake uses these same types of waves to push against the water, and some also push with their flattened tails.

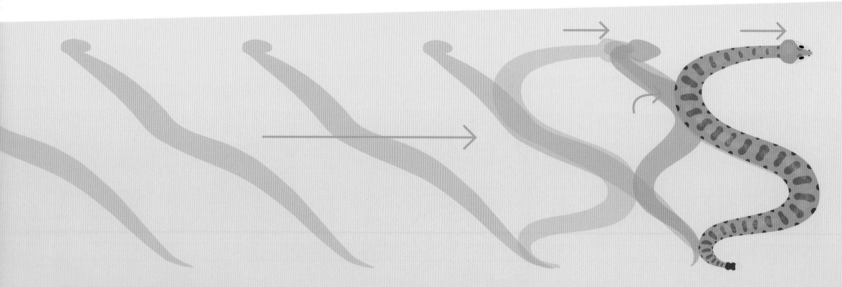

A SANDY SITUATION

A snake can't push against sand—the sand simply slips away. To get across these tricky spots (like rattlesnakes in a desert), the snake travels sideways instead. It lifts the front end of its body and plunks it back down a little bit to one side. It then does its usual S-shaped waves to bring its back half over to that side, too. This type of movement doesn't use a lot of energy, so it's a great way to go.

REAR, FRONT, REAR, FRONT

In tight spaces, like tunnels or grooves running up tree trunks, a snake travels by wedging itself in. It first folds up its tail, pushing the outside curves of its body against both sides of the space. Once it's safely tucked in, the snake stretches its head forward. It then S-shapes its front end until it's secure before pulling up its rear. Moving this way is an effective method when the snake's in a pinch—but it's exhausting!

SHIMMY THAT BELLY

It's not a quick way to travel, but some big, heavy snakes, like anacondas, move in a straight line. To do so, the snake's muscles make the skin on its belly move forward, and then the rest of its body glides after it.

CHILLAXING

Tree branches can be very thin, and snakes that spend time on them can be very heavy. To reduce the danger of falling, a snake stretches its long, skinny body across several branches to spread out its weight—like how people lie down to stop thin ice from cracking, rather than standing in one dangerous spot. To move from tree to tree, a snake can simply reach its body across the gap.

SHAPE-SHIFTER

Picture placing a small glob of runny jelly on a plate. Now tilt the plate. At the front end, the jelly runs downhill, dividing into several streams. At the back end, the jelly contracts. Through a microscope, that's what an amoeba on the move looks like. As it searches for food, it continually changes shape—the reason it was named after the Greek word for "change."

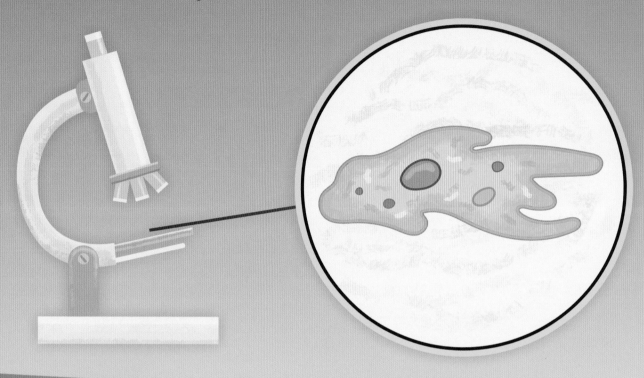

FALSE FEET

The tiny amoeba has only one cell: the basic building block of life. (In contrast, the human body is made up of about 37 trillion cells!) Some of its body can be firm like jelly and some of it can flow like liquid. To travel, it needs to use and overcome forces like thrust and friction just like any animal—but on a much smaller scale. Like a snail or snake, the amoeba doesn't have legs and feet. Instead, it extends parts of its body forward into "false feet," or pseudopodia. Its insides then flow into this space, emptying and bringing forward its rear end. Human white blood cells also move in this way.

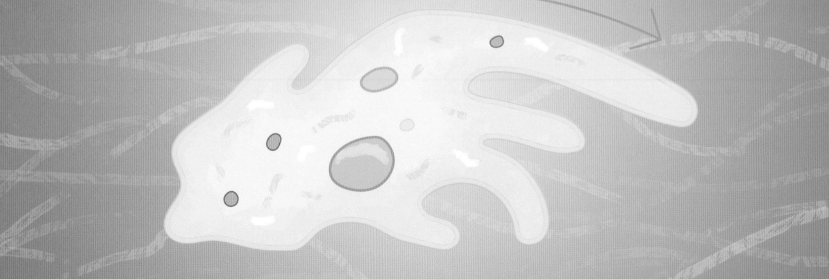

THAT-A-WAY!

Amoebas may look extremely simple, but they, too, need to eat. Without eyes or noses, how do they find food? They can sense the chemicals around them, traveling toward ones they like and away from ones they don't. If it happens to be food—tasty bacteria, for example, or algae—the amoeba extends a pseudopod toward it. This flows around the food, pulling it inside the amoeba so it can digest it.

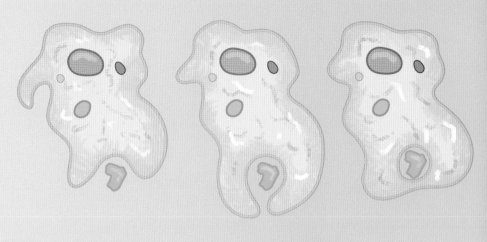

PUT ON SOME CLOTHES!

There are a couple of types of amoebas. Ones that live on or in the bodies of other animals are called parasitic. Most amoebas, though, live in places like soil or water. Because this type doesn't depend on other creatures, it's called free-living. Some free-living amoebas have hard shells made out of particles like sand and extend their pseudopodia through openings in these shells. Others are naked, meaning nothing protects their squishy bodies.

THE LONG AND THE SHORT

Not all one-celled organisms use pseudopodia to get around. Instead, some have long, hair-like structures that stick out, called flagella. To swim, they might move these flagella in a few ways— bending, rotating, or rowing. Other organisms have **shorter hairs on their bodies called cilia.** They use these hairs like rowboat **oars,** moving them in a specific pattern so they don't hit each other.

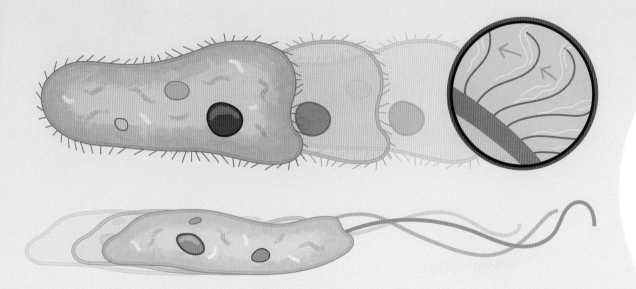

An **oar** is a type of lever used to propel and steer a boat through water.

CHAPTER THREE

GOING UP!
CLIMBING, SWINGING, AND JUMPING

Sometimes it's nice, or necessary, to get off the ground, especially if your food is up high or if something down low wants to eat you. Scooting up a tree is a great option, or even staying up there on a relatively permanent basis. Or maybe you're really small on the ground and a bigger, passing animal is your super tall target.

But take care—gravity wants to tug you back down! Luckily, many animals are built to cope with it. Here you'll meet super sticky geckos that can scurry up anything; gibbons who spend most of their lives up in the foliage and have amazing arms for swinging from branch to branch; and smaller-than-a-pencil-point fleas that think a cat, a dog, or even a person provides a wonderful place to settle in and feed on blood—and have an incredible ability to reach them.

Get ready. Get set. Jump!

GO, GECKO, GO

Scurry, scurry, scurry. Stop. *Scurry, scurry, scurry.* Stop. Under the moon, the gecko scoots through the gravel. Then it spies a tasty caterpillar way up in a tree. Gravity is no match for this little reptile—up it runs, sticking almost magically to the super smooth bark.

PERMANENT PUSH-UPS

Like on a spider or a crab, a gecko's legs jut out to the side. If we were built like this, we'd need a lot of muscle to hold ourselves up against gravity. (Think about doing a push-up. When you bend your arms, it's a lot of work. It's much easier if you straighten your arms and lock them beneath you.) But a gecko's legs work more like the legs of a carpenter's sawhorse, which act as **struts** to support whatever weight is on them. This setup makes the gecko very stable, great at turning, and less likely to fall backward off that tree trunk.

A **strut** is a brace that helps a structure stay strong.

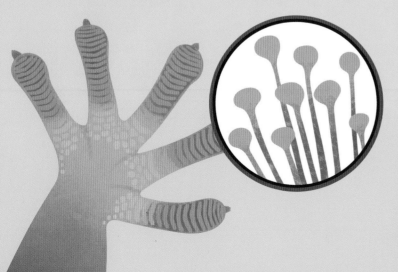

STICKY STUFF

Geckos can climb straight up smooth rocks and bark—and glass windows. That's because a gecko has incredibly fine hairs on its feet, and **each of these hairs branches into tiny spatula-like pads**. These pads flatten against the surface and attach to it thanks to very weak electrical forces. While these forces exist between any two objects that are super close, they're usually not strong enough to be sticky. But the gecko has an incredible number of pads, making the electrical forces for this creature even stronger than the tugging force of gravity.

PRACTICALLY USEFUL

A gecko's tail stores fat the animal can survive on if it can't find food. It can also detach when a predator tries to grab the gecko—and then the gecko simply grows a new one. Plus, a gecko can flick its tail while leaping from tree to tree to change the angle of its body and land upright—similar to how cheetahs use their tails for stability while steering.

REACHING FROM SIDE TO SIDE

As a gecko's front foot reaches forward, that side of its body stretches to help it reach even farther. Squishing its ribs on the opposite side, though, can make it difficult to breathe. That's one reason why a sprinting gecko stops to take breaks—it has to be still to catch its breath. This is the opposite of animals like horses. When a horse runs, its back undulates up and down, like a cheetah's S-shaped spine—not side to side. This actually helps the horse breathe while it's on the move. And remember those kangaroos and their bouncing organs!

IT'S SWING-TIME!

The gibbon hangs out—for real. With one of its hands hooked over a tree branch, its body dangles below. Gravity might want the animal to tumble down to where the predators are and the fruit isn't, but the gibbon is made to sway and swing.

LET'S BRACHIATE

Gibbons live in the tropical forests of southeastern Asia. To move quickly from tree to tree, a gibbon swings from hand to hand—a technique called brachiation. Lots of movements, like jumping, require creatures to bend body parts like knees to generate thrust, but the gibbon uses a different approach. It keeps its arms straight and relies on gravity to keep the swinging motion of its body going, like a **pendulum**. Even with that ability, though, sometimes gibbons fall!

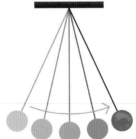

A **pendulum** is an object that swings from a fixed point with the help of gravity.

BUILT FOR SWINGING

Its small, light body and super long arms help a gibbon travel far and fast. It also has really flexible shoulder joints that rotate easily with each swing. Sometimes the gibbon grabs a new branch before letting go of the old one, or it can speed things up and launch itself into the air between grabs— like how humans switch between walking and running. And even though a gibbon's legs are way shorter than its arms, they matter, too. Just as you can pump your legs to go higher on a playground swing, a gibbon pumps its legs to speed up.

OTHER OPTIONS

A gibbon prefers to stay up and away from predators, but when it does come down to the ground, it walks on two feet just like a human. The big difference: the gibbon holds its arms up in the air for balance as it walks. When in the trees, the animal is also an impressive jumper—rather than swinging, it may leap to the next branch instead. (Too bad it can't just stretch across like a snake!)

IT'S ALL IN THE WRIST

Kids playing on monkey bars may look like great swingers, but a gibbon has an advantage: its one-of-a-kind wrist. Humans and other apes can rotate their wrists quite a bit, but a gibbon has a special type of joint in its wrist, like a shoulder joint, that can rotate even more. That's important when grabbing on to branches and flipping back off again. A gibbon's hands are also different. Its fingers and palms are super long so they can hook over the branches, and its thumbs are attached lower down so they can tuck safely out of the way.

A BOUNDING BLOODSUCKER

It's hard to be a flea when there's no food at flea level. Instead, the flea has to rocket itself high into the air to land on a passing blood-filled critter. How does a speck-size insect get up there? The trick is in the tension.

FLING THAT FLEA!

Gravity really wants objects to stick firmly to the ground. The issue for jumping creatures is to generate enough force to overcome that gravity and propel themselves upward and forward. Like a person, a flea prepares to jump by bending its legs. This movement squishes a block of **a rubbery substance called resilin** at the base of each hind leg, building tension. When the flea releases the pressure on the resilin, it springs back into its original shape, building thrust and shooting the bug into the air. The flea also pushes off with its toes. Take that, gravity!

CATCHY

A flea is covered with **tiny spines and hairs**. The ones on its hind legs grip the ground, creating friction and giving the flea something to push against so it can jump higher. Others snag on to the fur of the animal it lands on. Since these hairs point toward the rear of the flea, they don't get in the way when the flea crawls through the fur—but they do make it hard for the animal to remove the flea since they stick to fur like Velcro!

MADE FOR FUR

Not only is a flea an expert at jumping, it's an expert at crawling through thick fur. It has a flat, thin body and pointed head, which help it part the hairs. It doesn't have wings to get in the way, and its antennae lie back. The flea's body is also made of many movable segments, so it's flexible and can easily creep around obstacles. And its body is hard—perfect for protecting it from an itchy animal's teeth or claws.

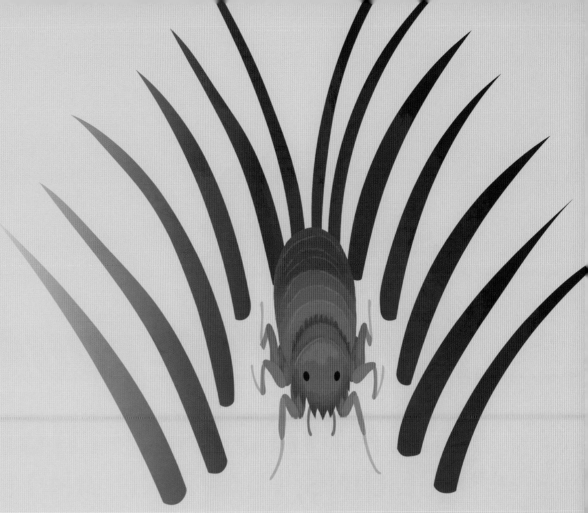

WHAT'S THAT CLICK?

Like a flea, a click beetle also builds up tension to jump—but not with its legs. When the beetle falls upside down, it arches its back. This causes **two tiny parts on its belly—a peg and the lip of a pit**—to catch on each other, building tension. When the catch releases, the beetle's body snaps upward and the insect is flung into the air (with a click!)—and hopefully lands right-side up. This trick would be handy for toppled tortoises, too!

CHAPTER FOUR

STAYING SKY-HIGH
GLIDING, FLAPPING, AND HOVERING

What a sweet life flying must be—high over the treetops with a stunning view of the world. Birds and insects reign where no person can go, at least not without some sort of contraption. But it's not always so easy for them either: remember those tough-to-beat forces like gravity and drag.

Lift and thrust to the rescue! Flying animals have built-in technologies and brilliant techniques for staying airborne. Some soar, spreading their wings and gliding as long as they can with the help of air currents. Think of ocean-living albatrosses. Others stay aloft with active flapping. Think of honking Canada geese. And others flap so fast and precisely they don't fly forward at all but stay in one place. Think of flower-sipping hoverflies.

Pick a method, and the sky's the limit!

SURFING THE WIND

Waves, waves, nothing but waves. There's no land in sight for the albatross. Will this huge bird get tired and plop into the ocean? Not likely. It rarely even flaps its wings, instead relying on the swoops of the wind.

GIVE ME A LIFT

Most birds flap to fly, but some, like the albatross, can fly while holding their wings still. Like a glider airplane, an albatross relies on the flow of air past its wings. Enough air has to flow past them, quickly enough, to give the bird enough lift to hold up its weight. The shape of the bird's wings and the angle the bird holds them at help make this happen. These also reduce drag so the bird can slice through the air.

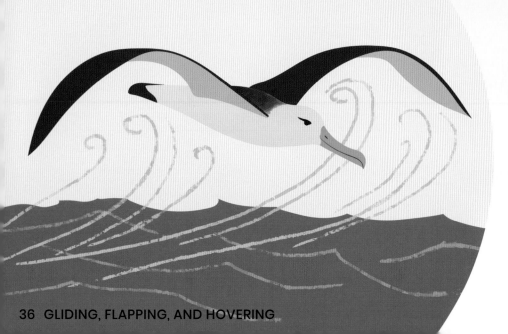

CATCHING A RIDE

Albatrosses are lucky the ocean is a windy place. This wind, slower close to the water and faster higher up, helps carry the albatross into the sky. Once there, the bird glides back downward. When it nearly reaches the water, it faces into the wind again—and back up it goes. By repeating this over and over, the albatross can fly huge distances over many hours while barely flapping its wings. Some other birds soar in a similar way along the windy sides of cliffs.

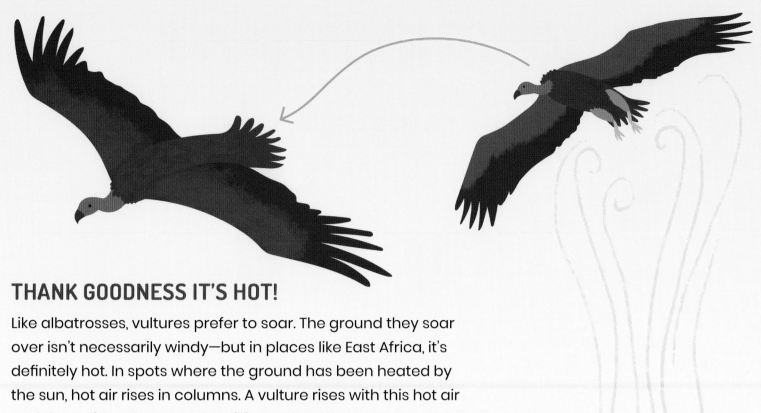

THANK GOODNESS IT'S HOT!

Like albatrosses, vultures prefer to soar. The ground they soar over isn't necessarily windy—but in places like East Africa, it's definitely hot. In spots where the ground has been heated by the sun, hot air rises in columns. A vulture rises with this hot air and then glides downward until it reaches the next hot patch. At night or on cool days, when these columns don't happen, vultures hang out on cliffs or in trees instead.

LOCKED IN PLACE

An albatross spends most of its life over the ocean, soaring for hundreds of thousands of kilometers every year. (It usually comes on land only to breed, where it often crash-lands.) To stay aloft for so long, it has a special **sheet of tendon** (the tissue that connects muscle to bone) in each shoulder, which locks its wing into place. That means the albatross doesn't have to use muscle power to keep its narrow wings fully spread, even though they're the longest wings of any bird.

A V-ERY GREAT WAY TO FLY

Honk, honk! Look up: the sky is full of Canada geese. They're on a long journey south, migrating thousands of kilometers to reach a warmer place to spend the winter. To fly for so long, they use powerful, rhythmic flaps. And that neatly spaced V isn't just for looks.

THE V-FACTOR

Flying in a neatly spaced V means Canada geese can easily watch and communicate with each other. The shape also saves energy. The goose at the front may do a lot of work, but each of the other geese benefits from the swirl of air created by the bird in front of it, which helps give it lift. These birds can fly much longer distances this way—all around their habitats in Canada and the United States. And when the lead goose gets tired, it drops back and lets another bird take a turn.

KEEP PUSHING

Like many birds, insects, and bats, a Canada goose flaps its wings to fly. Each stroke down pushes the air downward and backward, which provides the thrust to power the bird forward and the lift to keep it aloft. It then pulls its wings back up to get ready for the next push.

SHALL WE?

Canada geese are just as coordinated when they take off. Well before leaving the ground, a goose will tell the rest of its flock, which can range from a few birds to a thousand, that it intends to leave. It stretches its neck, shakes its head, flaps its wings, and walks in the direction it wants to go. Soon others join in, stretching and shaking and flapping, too. Eventually, they all understand it's time to take off.

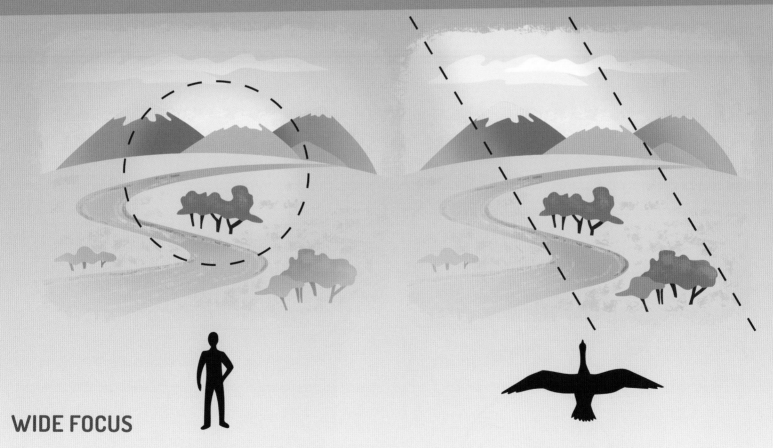

WIDE FOCUS

If a flying Canada goose had vision like ours, it could focus only on a tiny point of sky or land in front of it. Everything else would be blurry. Instead, the goose's eyes can focus along an entire line, not just one point. This means it can see both the sky and the ground clearly—along with any predators—while keeping track of the other geese in its flock.

A PRO AT STAYING PUT

Watch out, it's a wasp! No, wait—it's a harmless hoverfly. See how it hangs in the air by those flowers, suspended as if by an invisible thread? Its wings vibrating so quickly they blur, the insect uses special mechanisms and methods to barely move from its spot.

LIKE A HELICOPTER

Hoverflies are amazing at hovering. They can remain in one place mid-air for a while, like helicopters that rise and linger before zooming off. Similar to the rotor blades that push against the air and give the helicopter lift, the hoverfly's wings provide lift by moving in a figure eight, with an added twisting motion. By precisely controlling what its wings are doing, the insect can keep itself in the air without zipping away. Colorful, flower-sipping hummingbirds are masters at this, too.

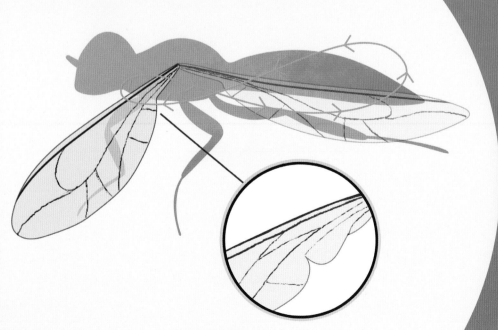

POWER AND PRECISION

To hover, a hoverfly flaps its wings hundreds of times per second. But the wings themselves have no muscles. Instead, they're powered by muscles that take up most of the fly's body. One group of muscles operates the wing's "hinges." These tiny, intricate parts connect the hoverfly's wings to its body. By changing what they do, the insect is able to steer. A tiny flap at the base of each wing, called the alula, also helps the insect turn.

LIKE A CAR AND A BIKE

A hoverfly is also like a car or a bicycle. First, it has a **clutch**. In some cars, this connects the power to the wheels. A hoverfly's two clutches connect its power to its wings. When the clutches are engaged, the wings flap. Disengaged, one or both wings stay still. The hoverfly also has **gears**. On a bicycle, these take the motion your feet create on the pedals and send it to the wheels—there are several gear choices so you can pedal comfortably. In a hoverfly, these gears control how far up and down its wings can move, helping it flap at an appropriate level of effort for the conditions around it or what it wants to do.

A **clutch** is a machine part that connects or disconnects the power from one part of an object to another.

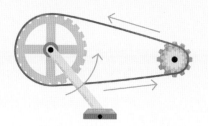

A **gear** is a machine part that transmits motion between parts of an object while controlling speed, force, and direction.

HALT! WHAT ARE THOSE?

Those club-like things sticking out behind the wings are called halteres. Like how a cheetah's inner ears tell it what position its head is in (same as ours), halteres tell a hoverfly what position its body is in. This information lets it adjust its movements to stay where it is, remain on course, or veer away. The halteres flap just like the wings but always in the opposite way, and help the hoverfly keep its flapping sense of rhythm.

CHAPTER FIVE

NO SINKING ALLOWED
ROWING, WALKING ON WATER, AND STAYING BUOYANT

Lakes, rivers, ponds. On hot summer days, it's fun to plunge right in. Open your eyes underwater and you might even see a fish.

Some water-loving animals, though, don't live in water. They spend at least some of their time on water or near its surface—either because they need to breathe fresh air or this is where they find their food. Gravity tries its best to sink them, but these creatures know how to rise above it.

Whirligig beetles don't need boats to stay afloat. Instead, their bodies act like miniature rowboats and their legs like oars, which use drag to create thrust. While hunting for food, fishing spiders take advantage of surface tension and walk on water.

And even if you do live in an ocean, do you have to be deep down all the time? The basking shark is a great example of an immense animal with a hidden feature that helps it stay buoyant and close to the surface.

Dive on in . . .

WHIRL, TWIRL, AND SWIRL

Some zip forward. Some turn left. Some speed about in a circle. It's a mass of whirligig beetles, zooming about on a pond. How do they sprint, steer, and prevent themselves from crashing? By rowing their bristly legs like oars to create useful drag on purpose.

ROW, ROW, ROW YOUR BOAT

To swim, a whirligig beetle uses its middle and hind legs like a rower uses a set of oars. Pulling the legs back creates drag, enabling the beetle to push against the water to generate forward thrust. When the insect moves the legs on each side of its body at the same time, it goes straight. When it uses them a little differently, the insect turns. With its body shaped like a boat, it can easily cut through the water, and floats thanks to hidden pockets of trapped air. Whirligigs and other water beetles aren't the only rowing creatures: some fish use their fins like oars, and ducks and beavers use their feet—and remember those single-celled organisms with cilia!

HAIRY LEGS

The bigger the oar's blade, the greater the drag it can create, which then generates better thrust. That's why whirligigs' middle and hind legs are **covered with many bristles** that spread out to make the legs bigger and create more drag. (Picture the way a swimmer pushes back with her arms and hands while doing the breaststroke.) When the whirligig's legs move forward again to prepare for the next push, the bristles fold in so the legs can move through the water with minimal drag. (Picture how the swimmer tucks her arms close to her chest as she prepares to extend them forward again.) But a whirligig doesn't use its front legs for swimming—they're for catching prey.

OXYGEN ON THE GO

Scare a whirligig and it might dive under the water. However, it doesn't hold its breath, and it also can't breathe like a fish. Instead, like a scuba diver, it brings along its own supply of oxygen by storing an air bubble by its wings, which are tucked under its back. The long-toed water beetle adapts in a different way—it covers its entire body in a thin layer of air, like a space suit, and can then live the rest of its life without surfacing again.

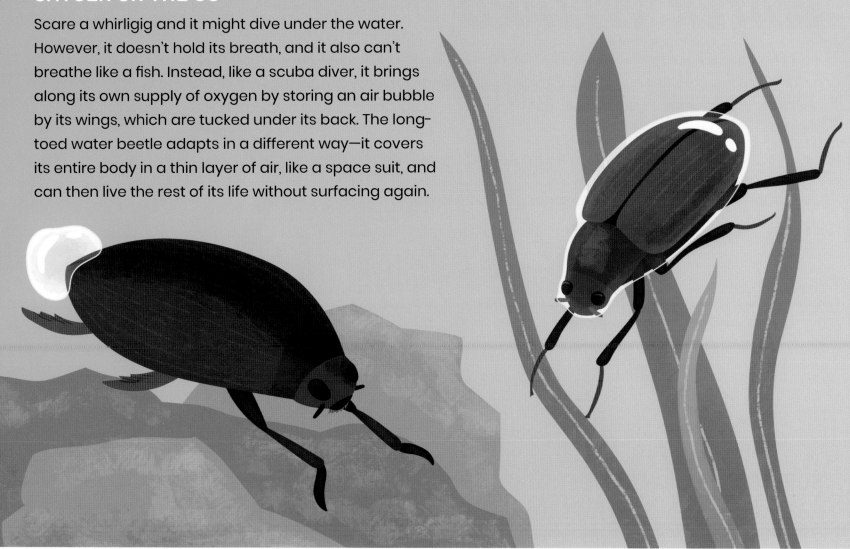

FOUR EYES ON THE LOOKOUT

A whirligig has four eyes: one pair for looking up to the sky and another for looking down into the water. This means that when it's swimming on the surface, the beetle can see all its surroundings, keeping it safe and helping it find food. The whirligig also has super sensitive antennae that sense the tiniest waves in the water, which might mean a delicious drowning insect is near.

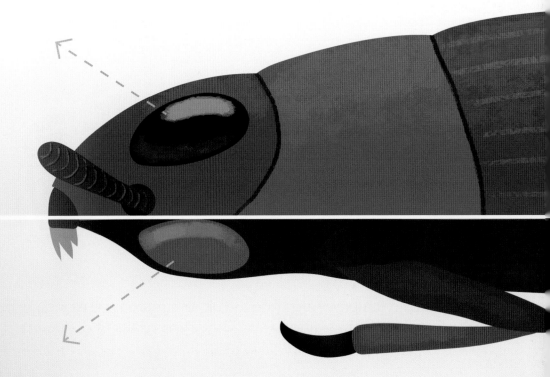

WATER WIZARD

Big, hairy lakeside spiders have a surprising habit—they like to eat fish. But swimming isn't their main way of getting to where the fish are. Instead, they have a wondrous, gravity-defying way of walking on the water until they find a yummy reason to dive.

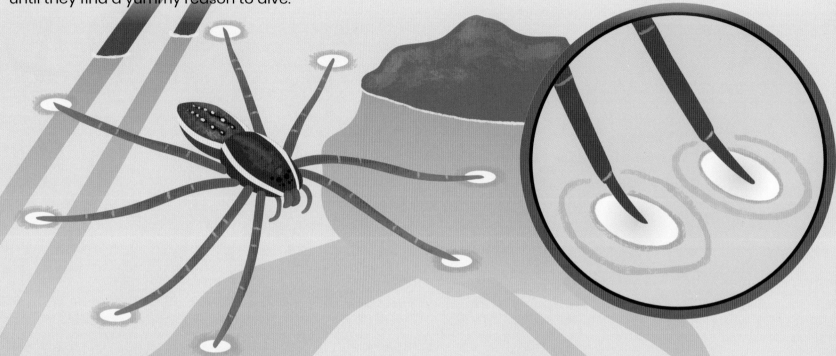

SURFACE-TENSION STRIDER

Even though a fishing spider can be as large as an adult's palm, it's still light enough to stand on the surface tension of the water—a right-side-up version of those underwater snails. Like the way a child's foot creates dimples in the surface of a trampoline, **the spider's feet create dimples in the surface tension**. The spider then uses these dimples like a whirligig beetle uses its legs: as oars. By pushing into the dimples to create drag, the spider generates the thrust it needs to walk. A basilisk lizard can cross water, too, by slapping the water with its feet while running really, really fast.

THE WINDY WAY

Rowing can take a lot of energy, so sometimes fishing spiders take it easy and leave the work to the wind. The spider lifts a couple of legs into the air, or stretches all its legs to push its body as high as it can above the water. This turns the spider into a kind of sail, allowing the wind to catch it and glide it across the surface until it decides to lower its legs or body and come to a stop.

HELPFUL HAIR

A fishing spider is very hairy—but not just for looks. Its **hairs are waxy and waterproof**, which means they stay dry and help the spider remain above water. (If something gets wet, it can easily break through the surface of the water. If something remains dry, it has more chances of floating on top.) The hairs also trap oxygen, so the spider can spend time underwater, like a whirligig, without coming up for air.

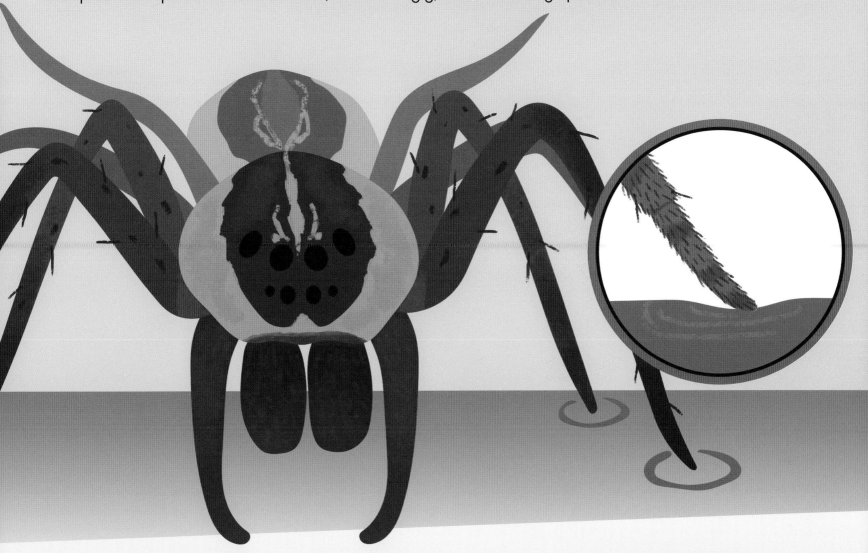

MOTION DETECTORS

A fishing spider uses its eight eyes to watch for fish swimming by or insects stuck to the water's surface. It also finds prey by using its hairs to sense vibrations in the water, similar to a whirligig's antennae. These tell the spider about the prey: what direction it's in, how far away it is, and even what type it is. The spider can then burst toward it, grab it with its legs, and paralyze it with its venom.

BIG MOUTH, BIGGER LIVER

The basking shark's mouth, ready for feeding, stretches in an enormous O. But if heavy objects sink in water—especially ones that are hauling water into themselves, too—why doesn't the huge shark? Give credit to a fatty liver—one of several ways aquatic animals remain bobbingly buoyant.

THAT'S SOME LIVER

A basking shark can weigh as much as an elephant and stretch as long as a bus, making it the second-largest fish after whale sharks. It also has **a huge liver filled with an oily substance** that's less dense (less compact) than the surrounding water. In water, items that are less dense than the water will float to the surface, and items that are more dense will sink. The basking shark's oily liver acts like a lifejacket that creates buoyancy and helps the animal bob up. But its big body also makes it a slow swimmer. Other sharks, like the ones that chase seals, can't afford to be so slow. Instead of having huge livers, they have to keep swimming to stop from sinking.

TAKE YOUR PICK

An oily liver isn't the only way to stay buoyant. Some fish, like goldfish or cod, have swim bladders. These inner spaces are filled with gases and also act like lifejackets. The hard-shelled pearly nautilus and cuttlefish have chambers filled with gas. Jellyfish and squid have salty jellies and liquids in them that are less dense than water. Light-producing lantern fish and ancient coelacanths, which were already around at the time of the dinosaurs, have floats filled with fatty wax.

USE THAT NOSE

A basking shark swims with its mouth wide open—that's how it filters out and eats drifting plankton, the tiny plants and animals that drift on or near the water's surface. Sharks like great whites must think hard to hunt animals like seals, so they have relatively big brains. But sifting out plankton is simple, so the basking shark has a tiny brain—and a huge nose. A big part of its head is devoted to sniffing that plankton out. For the basking shark, a sense of smell is more important than a sense of smarts.

MEGA-SANDPAPER

To swimming people, the most dangerous part of a basking shark is its skin. That's because the fish is covered with sharp scales that protect it from predators like killer whales and other sharks. Most sharks' scales are slicked backward, giving protection while helping the shark glide forward silently with minimal drag—swimsuits have even been made out of fabric that mimics this skin. The basking shark, though, doesn't need to move fast, so its scales poke out every which way.

49

CHAPTER SIX

UNDERWATER EXPERTS
UNDULATING, USING HYDROFOILS, AND SHOOTING WITH JET PROPULSION

Humans aren't made to live in water, but we sure have figured out a lot of ways to swim through it: the front crawl, backstroke, breaststroke, butterfly . . . and even the doggy paddle.

But have you heard about the "triggerfish ripple," the "penguin flap," or the "squid squirt"—all proven methods to keep from sinking, fight drag, and advance through thick water?

No, these aren't real swimming styles, at least not for people. But triggerfish do ripple their fins to steer among tricky reefs. Penguins do flap their wings, even when submerged in ice-cold oceans. And squid do rapidly squirt water out of their bodies to blast forward like rocket ships—occasionally even shooting into the sky.

Three, two, one—swim!

FUNCTIONAL FLOWY FINS

Snap. Snap. Who's that skinny fish with the big lips and sharp, nipping teeth? A triggerfish, weaving its way through thin passageways in a maze of coral. Luckily, it knows how to get around precisely and safely, undulating its fins to escape bigger fish and find its own crunchy snacks.

THE RIPPLE EFFECT

To hunt and hide within coral reefs, a fish has to be good at maneuvering. A triggerfish has several fins, but the main ones it uses are the big matching ones on its belly and at the rear end of its back, near its tail.

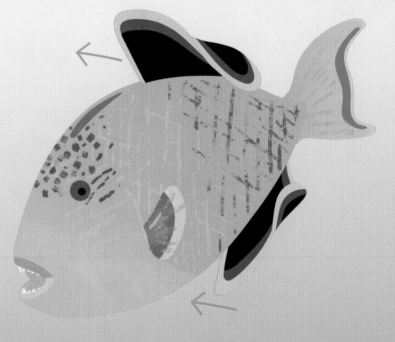

By undulating these fins—as if a wave is rippling through them—the fish pushes against the water to create lift and thrust.

HOW THE TRIGGERFISH GOT ITS NAME

The front fin on a triggerfish's back is actually **three spines**. When the fish wants to stay safe, it tucks itself into a crack and locks the front, biggest spine upright. This makes it really hard for a predator to tug the fish out. Once the triggerfish deems it safe and wants to swim free again, it needs to unlock the big spine. To do so, it withdraws the second, middle spine, which **triggers the big spine to unlock**. This action is how the fish got its name.

REALLY BIG FINS

For an extreme example of fins that undulate, look at a ray. A ray kind of looks like a big pancake, but that's actually its body and two very large fins. Some types of rays undulate these fins like triggerfish, while others flap them like birds. Electric rays prefer to move their tail fins to generate thrust and lift. Like basking sharks, rays have oily livers that help them float—but not super big ones. If they stop swimming, they start sinking. That's okay, though, since they like burying themselves in the seafloor sand.

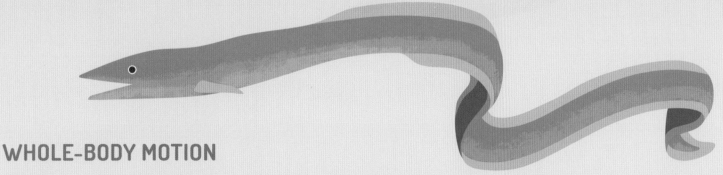

WHOLE-BODY MOTION

Many other types of fish, like eels, move their whole bodies and tails instead of their fins. While an eel has long, thin fins that run the length of its body, its body movements are what matter. Like a snake, an eel forms S-shaped waves that push against the water and propel it forward. Generally, the waves start small by the head but get bigger by the time they get to the tail. Sea snakes and crocodiles also do this body-tail shimmy.

FLYING THROUGH WATER

Waddle, waddle, flop. Swish, swoosh, splash. While a penguin moves awkwardly on land, rocking from foot to foot and slip-sliding on its belly, this bird becomes graceful once it plunges into the ocean. Gravity and drag are no match for the power of its made-for-water wings.

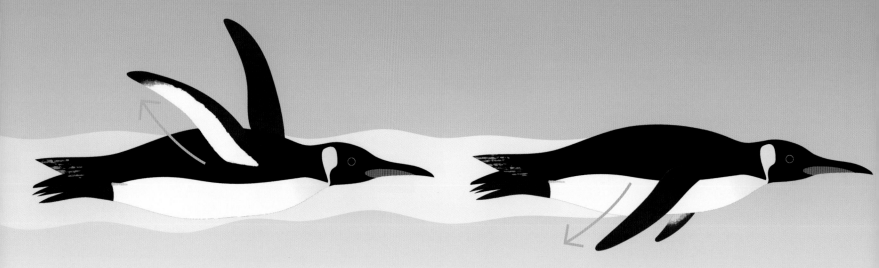

THE PUSH AND THE PULL

A penguin spends about three-quarters of its life in water. There, it flaps its wings like a bird in the sky—but they push against water, not air. The penguin uses its paddle-like wings as **hydrofoils** to create lift and thrust, like a ship's propellers. But while a bird in the sky can easily pull its wings up after a push down, a penguin in water has to use a lot of power to flap up and down. So its wing-lifting muscles are bigger than other birds'.

IT'S A PORPOISE—A DOLPHIN—A PENGUIN!

Like porpoises and dolphins, penguins sometimes leap out of the water. Since air has less drag than water, this helps them save energy. It also lets them grab a breath, escape predators, or get onto ice or land. While speeding up to leap, a penguin's body releases tiny bubbles of air trapped in its feathers. Some researchers think this little coating of air makes it easier to zip through the water and burst out.

SHAPED FOR SWIMMING

A penguin has a bullet-shaped body, tucks its head near its shoulders while swimming, and coats its feathers with a special oil. These help it move through the water with minimal drag. Also, its legs and webbed feet are positioned really far back on its body. On land, this means it waddles strangely. But in the water, it can easily tuck its legs by its tail, staying streamlined while using them as rudders to steer.

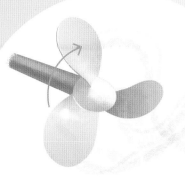

Like each blade of a ship's propeller, a **hydrofoil** is a flat surface used underwater to produce lift and thrust for an object.

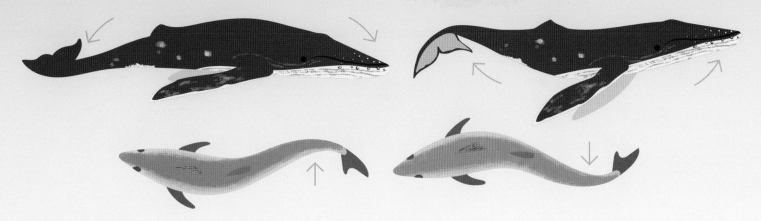

A TALE ABOUT TAILS

Like a penguin beats its wings, many sea creatures use hydrofoils to swim. A marine turtle, for example, beats its flippers. Many other animals use their tails—like how people wear flippers to swim faster. Whales beat their tail fins up and down, while tuna beat them side to side. Lots of tail movement is a great way to swim fast. And lots of animals move their fins and undulate their bodies, like sharks. In fact, most sea animals use a fin/body combo.

THE SPACESHIP OF THE SEA

A squid may look like a rubbery blob and tangle of ropes, but it has the same need to escape from predators and find food as any other creature. How does it create the thrust to move? The secret lies in the squirt.

BALLOON BODY

A squid is like a jet airplane, a rocket ship—and a balloon. Fill a balloon with air and then suddenly let the air go—the balloon splutters away. Rather than air, though, a squid fills up a special space in its body with water and then squirts the water back out. This "jet propulsion" is also how jet airplanes and rocket ships shoot forward, by ejecting gas instead of water. The squid may squirt quickly or slowly to go different speeds. Its gills are also in this space, so this is how the squid breathes.

SLOW, STEADY, AND STREAMLINED

A gentler way to move is by swishing its two fins. Some squid do this by flapping them up and down like a Canada goose's wings; others undulate them like a triggerfish's fins. When jetting fast, the squid wraps these fins against its body and out of the way. The squid also tucks its 10 tentacles and arms together to stay streamlined; while not jetting, the squid uses these arms and tentacles to catch prey and draw it into its bird-like beak. And where exactly is the squid's head? There, between the arms, which is why squid are a type of cephalopod, which means "head foot."

CAN'T CATCH ME!

Jetting is a quick way to escape predators like sharks, but a squid also has many other means of defense. It can change color or pattern to blend into the background. To confuse predators, it can squirt dark ink or create its own distracting light. It may release a poison. Or, if caught in a tussle, the squid can break off an arm or two to escape—and eventually grow new ones back, like a gecko does with its tail. Another type of cephalopod, the octopus, can also do these things.

IT'S A PORPOISE—A DOLPHIN— A PENGUIN—A SQUID!

To escape predators or maybe save energy, a squid may leap into the air—and almost, for a few moments, fly. To do so, the squid jets so forcefully it shoots itself out of the water. But unlike penguins that often burst out of the ocean to get onto land, the squid stays skyborne. It spreads its fins and arms, which have webbing between them, like wings. It may also flap its fins while it's up there or do more jet propulsion. Finally, it tucks its fins and arms away and dives back into the water.

CONCLUSION
THE NEXT STEP

The next time you're outside, watch a bird. Is it flapping its wings? Or gliding on air currents? How does that bird move differently than the next bird you see? How do they both move the same as an airplane—or not?

Now, if there's a squirrel around, take a look at it. How does it dash up and down a tree with ease, while cats sometimes get stuck on high branches? (Spoiler alert: The squirrel can rotate its feet so its claws always get a good grip. Cats can't do this, so their claws aren't as useful when the animal tries to come down.) Yup, this is another example of gravity and friction in action!

In fact, check out whatever animals are around you, whether you live on a mountain, in a city, or by the ocean. Consider why they're moving—to feed? to flee? Do they go about it in ways you haven't paid attention to before? Do they have unique body parts? How are they creating lift or producing thrust? What forces are working for and against them?

Many millions of animals live on Earth—some researchers say there are as many as 7.7 million species! That means there are millions of ways their movements can astound us.

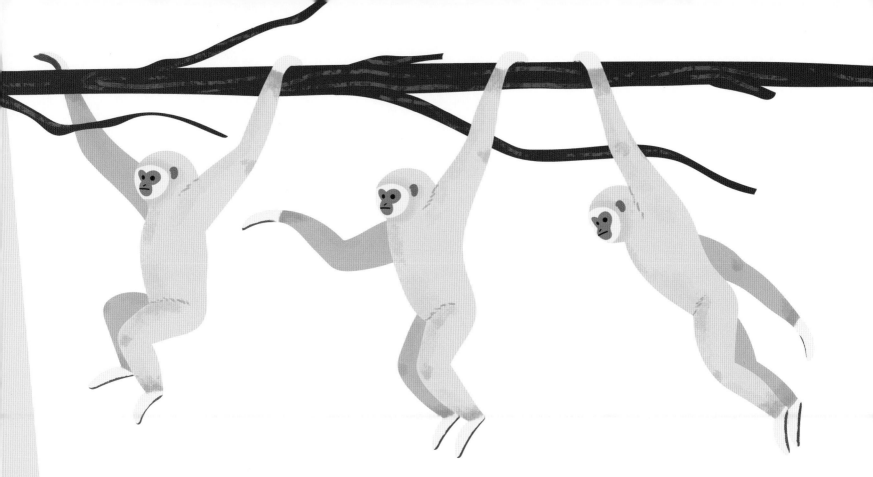

And the study of biomechanics isn't just fascinating—it can also be functional. By analyzing kangaroo hops, researchers have been able to make better prosthetic legs. Gecko feet can teach us how to hang on to a spaceship while repairing it—or even help us hang a TV on a wall. Large tankers and cruise ships use bubbly coatings to reduce drag, just like penguins. Researchers are creating robots that can handle different terrains by moving in all sorts of animal-like ways: like snails on water, snakes in narrow spaces, or gibbons swinging up high.

Maybe one day you'll be a coach and can use your knowledge about animals to help athletes perform better. Maybe you'll work in movies and make super realistic wildlife special effects. Maybe you'll design a robot that can navigate a cluttered home to help a senior live an easier life. If shark scales can inspire swimsuits, just think of all the innovations still to be imagined!

Keep wondering . . . keep watching . . . keep learning!

SELECT SOURCES

The information in this book came from many sources, from scientific studies to correspondence with experts. However, the backbone of it came from one British zoologist and biomechanics expert who dedicated himself to helping people understand how animals move. His name was Robert McNeill Alexander. Here are the books of his I consulted:

- *Locomotion of Animals*. Glasgow: Blackie & Son Ltd., 1982.

- *Exploring Biomechanics: Animals in Motion*. New York: Scientific American Library, 1992.

- *Principles of Animal Locomotion*. Princeton, New Jersey, and Woodstock, Oxfordshire: Princeton University Press, 2006.

ACKNOWLEDGMENTS

Thank you to Samantha Dixon for her colorful and eye-catching illustrations, which have helped bring these amazing animals to life, and to the team at Annick Press, particularly Claire Caldwell, Katie Hearn, Kaela Cadieux, Mary Ann Blair, DoEun Kwon, and Paul Covello. Also a big hug to my agent Hilary McMahon at Westwood Creative Artists.

Thumbs-up to all the experts who helped ensure the information in this book is correct: Kellar Autumn, Andrew Biewener, Malcolm Burrows, Young-Hui Chang, Mark Denny, Frank Fish, Bruce Jayne, Robert Kay, John Long, Crystal Maier, Linnea van Griethuijsen, Kim Ryall Woolcock—and particularly Rodger Kram. Any mistakes are my own.

And a final nod to the librarians at my local library, and libraries beyond, who helped me connect with the information I needed.

INDEX